A History of Aeronautics
Part II

AF729080

By

W. Lockwood Marsh And Evelyn Charles Vivian

Double9 BOOKS

A History of Aeronautics
Part II
by W. Lockwood Marsh And Evelyn Charles Vivian

ISBN: 978-93-62767-74-5

Published by

DOUBLE 9 BOOKS
2/13-B, Ansari Road
Daryaganj, New Delhi – 110002
info@double9books.com
www.double9books.com
Tel. 011-40042856

About the same time that the Wrights were carrying out their power-driven experiments, a band of pioneers was quite independently beginning to approach success in France. In practically every case, however, they started from a somewhat different standpoint and took as their basic idea the cellular (or box) kite. This form of kite, consisting of two superposed surfaces connected at each end by a vertical panel or curtain of fabric, had proved extremely successful for man-carrying purposes, and, therefore, it was little wonder that several minds conceived the idea of attempting to fly by fitting a series of box-kites with an engine. The first to achieve success was M. Santos-Dumont, the famous Brazilian pioneer-designer of airships, who, on November 12th, 1906, made several flights, the last of which covered a little over 700 feet. Santos-Dumont's machine consisted essentially of two box-kites, forming the main wings, one on each side of the body, in which the pilot stood, and at the front extremity of which was another movable box-kite to act as elevator and rudder. The curtains at the ends were intended to give lateral stability, which was further ensured by setting the wings slightly inclined upwards from the centre, so that when seen from the front they formed a wide V. This feature is still to be found in many aeroplanes to-day and has come to be known as the 'dihedral.' The motor was at first of 24 horse-power, for which later a 50 horse-power Antoinette engine was substituted; whilst a three-wheeled undercarriage was provided, so that the machine could start without external mechanical aid. The machine was constructed of bamboo and steel, the weight being as low as 352 lbs. The span was 40 feet, the length being 33 feet, with a total surface of main planes of 860 square feet. It will thus be seen—for comparison with the Wright machine—that the weight per horse-power (with the 50 horse-power engine) was only 7 lbs., while the wing loading was equally low at 1/2 lb. per square foot.

The main features of the Santos-Dumont machine were the box-kite form of construction, with a dihedral angle on the main planes, and the forward elevator which could be moved in any direction and therefore acted in the same way as the rudder at the rear of the Wright biplane. It had a single propeller revolving in the centre behind the wings and was fitted with an undercarriage incorporated in the machine.

The other chief French experimenters at this period were the Voisin Freres, whose first two machines—identical in form—were sold to Delagrange and H. Farman, which has sometimes caused confusion, the two purchasers being credited with the design they bought. The Voisins, like the Wrights, based their designs largely on the experimental work of Lilienthal, Langley, Chanute, and others, though they also carried out tests on the lifting properties of aerofoils in a wind tunnel of their own. Their first machines, like those of Santos-Dumont, showed the effects of experimenting with box-kites, some of which they had built for M. Ernest Archdeacon in 1904. In their case the machine, which was again a biplane, had, like both the others previously mentioned, an elevator in front—though in this case of monoplane form—and, as in the Wright, a rudder was fitted in rear of the main planes. The Voisins, however, fitted a fixed biplane horizontal 'tail'—in an effort to obtain a measure of automatic longitudinal stability—between the two surfaces of which the single rudder worked. For lateral stability they depended entirely on end curtains between the upper and lower surfaces of both the main planes and biplane tail surfaces. They, like Santos-Dumont, fitted a wheeled undercarriage, so that the machine was self-contained. The Voisin machine, then, was intended to be automatically stable in both senses; whereas the Wrights deliberately produced a machine which was entirely dependent upon the pilot's skill for its stability. The dimensions of the Voisin may be given for comparative purposes, and were as follows: Span 33 feet with a chord (width from back to front) of main planes of 6 1/2 feet, giving a total area of 430 square feet. The 50 horse-power Antoinette engine, which was enclosed in the body (or 'nacelle ') in the front of which the pilot sat, drove a propeller behind, revolving between the outriggers carrying the tail. The total weight, including Farman as pilot, is given as 1,540 lbs., so that the machine was much heavier than either of the others; the weight per horse-power being midway between the Santos-Dumont and the Wright at 31 lbs. per square foot, while the wing loading was considerably greater than either at 3 1/2 lbs. per square foot. The Voisin machine was experimented with by Farman and Delagrange from about June 1907 onwards, and was in the subsequent years developed by Farman; and right up to the commencement of the War upheld the principles of the box-kite method of construction for training purposes. The chief modification of the original design was the addition of flaps (or ailerons) at the rear extremities of the main planes to give lateral control, in a manner analogous to the wing-warping method invented by the Wrights, as a result of which the end curtains between the planes were abolished. An additional elevator was fitted at the rear of the fixed biplane tail, which eventually led to the discarding of the front elevator altogether. During the same period the Wright machine came into line with the others by the fitting of a wheeled undercarriage integral with the machine. A fixed horizontal tail was also added to the rear rudder, to which a movable elevator was later attached; and, finally, the front elevator was done away with. It will thus be seen that having started from the very different standpoints of automatic stability and complete control by the pilot, the Voisin (as developed in the Farman) and Wright machines, through gradual evolution finally resulted in aeroplanes of similar characteristics embodying a modicum of both features.

Before proceeding to the next stage of progress mention should be made of the experimental work of Captain Ferber in France. This officer carried out a large number of experiments with gliders contemporarily with the Wrights, adopting—like them—the Chanute biplane principle. He adopted the front elevator from the Wrights, but immediately went a step farther by also fitting a fixed tail in rear, which did not become a feature of the Wright machine until some seven or eight years later. He built and appeared to have flown a machine fitted with a motor in 1905, and was commissioned to go to America by the French War Office on a secret mission to the Wrights. Unfortunately, no complete account of his experiments appears to exist, though it can be said that his work was at least as important as that of any of the other pioneers mentioned.

II
MULTIPLICITY OF IDEAS

In a review of progress such as this, it is obviously impossible, when a certain stage of development has been reached, owing to the very multiplicity of experimenters, to continue dealing in anything approaching detail with all the different types of machines; and it is proposed, therefore, from this point to deal only with tendencies, and to mention individuals merely as examples of a class of thought rather than as personalities, as it is often difficult fairly to allocate the responsibility for any particular innovation.

During 1907 and 1908 a new type of machine, in the monoplane, began to appear from the workshops of Louis Bleriot, Robert Esnault-Pelterie, and others, which was destined to give rise to long and bitter controversies on the relative advantages of the two types, into which it is not proposed to enter here; though the rumblings of the conflict are still to be heard by discerning ears. Bleriot's early monoplanes had certain new features, such as the location of the pilot, and in some cases the engine, below the wing; but in general his monoplanes, particularly the famous No. XI on which the first Channel crossing was made on July 25th, 1909, embodied the main principles of the Wright and Voisin types, except that the propeller was in front of instead of behind the supporting surfaces, and was, therefore, what is called a 'tractor' in place of the then more conventional 'pusher.' Bleriot aimed at lateral balance by having the tip of each wing pivoted, though he soon fell into line with the Wrights and adopted the warping system. The main features of the design of Esnault-Pelterie's monoplane was the inverted dihedral (or kathedral as this was called in Mr S. F. Cody's British Army Biplane of 1907) on the wings, whereby the tips were considerably lower than the roots at the body. This was designed to give automatic lateral stability, but, here again, conventional practice was soon adopted and the R.E.P. monoplanes, which became well-known in this country through their adoption in the early days by Messrs Vickers, were of the ordinary monoplane design, consisting of a tractor propeller with wire-stayed wings, the pilot being in an enclosed fuselage containing the engine in front and carrying at its rear extremity fixed horizontal and vertical surfaces combined with movable elevators and rudder. Constructionally, the R.E.P. monoplane was of extreme interest as the body was constructed of steel. The Antoinette monoplane, so ably flown by Latham, was another very famous machine of the 1909-1910 period, though its performance were frequently marred by engine failure; which was indeed the bugbear of all these early experimenters, and it is difficult to say, after this lapse of time, how far in many cases the failures which occurred, both in performances and even in the actual ability to rise from the ground, were due to defects in design or merely faults in the primitive engines available. The Antoinette aroused admiration chiefly through its graceful, birdlike lines, which have probably never been equalled; but its chief interest for our present purpose lies in the novel method of wing-staying which was employed. Contemporary monoplanes practically all had their wings stayed by wires to a post in the centre above the fuselage, and, usually, to the undercarriage below. In the Antoinette, however, a king post was introduced half-way along the wing, from which wires were carried to the ends of the wings and the body. This was intended to give increased strength and permitted of a greater wing-spread and consequently improved aspect ratio. The same system of construction was adopted in the British Martinsyde monoplanes of two or three years later.

This period also saw the production of the first triplane, which was built by A. V. Roe in England and was fitted with a J.A.P. engine of only 9 horse-power—an amazing performance which remains to this day unequalled. Mr Roe's triplane was chiefly interesting otherwise for the method of maintaining longitudinal control, which was achieved by pivoting the whole of the three main planes so that their angle of incidence could be altered. This was the direct converse of the universal practice of elevating by means of a subsidiary surface either in front or rear of the main planes.

Recollection of the various flying meetings and exhibitions which one attended during the years from 1909 to 1911, or even 1912 are chiefly notable for the fact that the first thought on seeing any new type of machine was not as to what its 'performance'—in speed, lift, or what not—would be; but speculation as to whether it would leave the ground at all when eventually tried. This is perhaps the best indication of the outstanding characteristic of that interim period between the time of the first actual flights and the later period, commencing about 1912, when ideas had become settled and it was at last becoming possible to forecast on the drawing-board the performance of the completed machine in the air. Without going into details, for which there is no space here, it is difficult to convey the correct impression of the chaotic state which existed as to even the elementary principles of aeroplane design. All the exhibitions contained large numbers—one had almost written a majority—of machines which embodied the most unusual features and which never could, and in practice never did, leave the ground. At the same time, there were few who were sufficiently hardy to say certainly that this or that innovation was wrong; and consequently dozens of inventors in every country were conducting isolated experiments on both good and bad lines. All kinds of devices, mechanical and otherwise, were claimed as the solution of the problem of stability, and there was even controversy as to whether any measure of stability was not undesirable; one school maintaining that the only safety lay in the pilot having the sole say in the attitude of the machine at any given moment, and fearing danger from the machine having any mind of its own, so to speak. There was, as in most controversies, some right on both sides, and when we come to consider the more settled period from 1912 to the outbreak of the War in 1914 we shall find how a compromise was gradually effected.

At the same time, however, though it was at the time difficult to pick out, there was very real progress being made, and, though a number of 'freak' machines fell out by the wayside, the pioneer designers of those days learnt by a process of trial and error the right principles to follow and gradually succeeded in getting their ideas crystallised.

In connection with stability mention must be made of a machine which was evolved in the utmost secrecy by Mr J. W. Dunne in a remote part of Scotland under subsidy from the War office. This type, which was constructed in both monoplane and biplane form, showed that it was in fact possible in 1910 and 1911 to design an aeroplane which could definitely be left to fly itself in the air. One of the Dunne machines was, for example flown from Farnborough to Salisbury Plain without any control other than the rudder being touched; and on another occasion it flew a complete circle with all controls locked automatically assuming the correct bank for the radius of turn. The peculiar form of wing used, the camber of which varied from the root to the tip, gave rise however, to a certain loss in efficiency, and there was also a difficulty in the pilot assuming adequate control when desired. Other machines designed to be stable—such as the German Etrich and the British Weiss gliders and Handley-Page monoplanes—were based on the analogy of a wing attached to a certain seed found in Nature (the 'Zanonia' leaf), on the righting effect of back-sloped wings combined with upturned (or 'negative') tips. Generally speaking, however, the machines of the 1909-1912 period relied for what automatic stability they had on the principle of the dihedral angle, or flat V, both longitudinally and laterally. Longitudinally this was obtained by setting the tail at a slightly smaller angle than the main planes.

The question of reducing the resistance by adopting 'stream-line' forms, along which the air could flow uninterruptedly without the formation of eddies, was not at first properly realised, though credit should be given to Edouard Nieuport, who in 1909 produced a monoplane with a very large body which almost completely enclosed the pilot and made the machine very fast, for those days, with low horse-power. On one of these machines C. T. Weyman won the Gordon-Bennett Cup for America in 1911 and another put up a fine performance in the same race with only a 30 horse-power engine. The subject, was however, early taken up by the British Advisory Committee for Aeronautics, which was established by the Government in 1909, and designers began to realise the importance of streamline struts and fuselages towards the end of this transition period. These efforts were at first not always successful and showed at times a lack of understanding of the problems involved, but there was a very marked improvement during the year 1912. At the Paris Aero Salon held early in that year there was a notable variety of ideas on the subject; whereas by the time of the one held in October designs had considerably settled down, more than one exhibitor showing what were called 'monocoque' fuselages completely circular in shape and having very low resistance, while the same show saw the introduction of rotating cowls over the propeller bosses, or 'spinners,' as they came to be called during the War. A particularly fine example of stream-lining was to be found in the Deperdussin monoplane on which Vedrines won back the Gordon-Bennett Aviation Cup from America at a speed of 105.5 m.p.h.—a considerable improvement on the 78 m.p.h. of the preceding year, which was by no means accounted for by the mere increase in engine power from 100 horse-power to 140 horse-power. This machine was the first in which the refinement of 'stream-lining' the pilot's head, which became a feature of subsequent racing machines, was introduced. This consisted of a circular padded excresence above the cockpit immediately behind the pilot's head, which gradually tapered off into the top surface of the fuselage. The object was to give the air an uninterrupted flow instead of allowing it to be broken up into eddies behind the head of the pilot, and it also provided a support against the enormous wind-pressure encountered. This true stream-line form of fuselage owed its introduction to the Paulhan-Tatin 'Torpille' monoplane of the Paris Salon of early 1917. Altogether the end of the year 1912 began to see the disappearance of 'freak' machines with all sorts of original ideas for the increase of stability and performance. Designs had by then gradually become to a considerable extent standardised, and it had become unusual to find a machine built which would fail to fly. The Gnome engine held the field owing to its advantages, as the first of the rotary type, in lightness and ease of fitting into the nose of a fuselage. The majority of machines were tractors (propeller in front) although a preference, which died down subsequently, was still shown for the monoplane over the biplane. This year also saw a great increase in the number of seaplanes, although the 'flying boat' type had only appeared at intervals and the vast majority were of the ordinary aeroplane type fitted with floats in place of the land undercarriage; which type was at that time commonly called 'hydro-aeroplane.' The usual horse power was 50—that of the smallest Gnome engine—although engines of 100 to 140 horse-power were also fitted occasionally. The average weight per horse-power varied from 18 to 25 lbs., while the wing-loading was usually in the neighbourhood of 5 to 6 lbs. per square foot. The average speed ranged from 65-75 miles per hour.

III
PROGRESS ON STANDARDISED LINES

In the last section an attempt has been made to show how, during what was from the design standpoint perhaps the most critical period, order gradually became evident out of chaos, ill-considered ideas dropped out through failure to make good, and, though there was still plenty of room for improvement in details, the bulk of the aeroplanes showed a general similarity in form and conception. There was still a great deal to be learnt in finding the best form of wing section, and performances were still low; but it had become definitely possible to say that flying had emerged from the chrysalis stage and had become a science. The period which now began was one of scientific development and improvement—in performance, manoeuvrability, and general airworthiness and stability.

The British Military Aeroplane Competition held in the summer of 1912 had done much to show the requirements in design by giving possibly the first opportunity for a definite comparison of the performance of different machines as measured by impartial observers on standard lines—albeit the methods of measuring were crude. These showed that a high speed—for those days—of 75 miles an hour or so was attended by disadvantages in the form of an equally fast low speed, of 50 miles per hour or more, and generally may be said to have given designers an idea what to aim for and in what direction improvements were required. In fact, the most noticeable point perhaps of the machines of this time was the marked manner in which a machine that was good in one respect would be found to be wanting in others. It had not yet been possible to combine several desirable attributes in one machine. The nearest approach to this was perhaps to be found in the much discussed Government B.E.2 machine, which was produced from the Royal Aircraft Factory at Farnborough, in the summer of 1912. Though considerably criticized from many points of view it was perhaps the nearest approach to a machine of all-round efficiency that had up to that date appeared. The climbing rate, which subsequently proved so important for military purposes, was still low, seldom, if ever, exceeding 400 feet per minute; while gliding angles (ratio of descent to forward travel over the ground with engine stopped) little exceeded 1 in 8.

The year 1912 and 1913 saw the subsequently all-conquering tractor biplane begin to come into its own. This type, which probably originated in England, and at any rate attained to its greatest excellence prior to the War from the drawing offices of the Avro Bristol and Sopwith firms, dealt a blow at the monoplane from which the latter never recovered.

The two-seater tractor biplane produced by Sopwith and piloted by H. G. Hawker, showed that it was possible to produce a biplane with at least equal speed to the best monoplanes, whilst having the advantage of greater strength and lower landing speeds. The Sopwith machine had a top speed of over 80 miles an hour while landing as slowly as little more than 30 miles an hour; and also proved that it was possible to carry 3 passengers with fuel for 4 hours' flight with a motive power of only 80 horse-power. This increase in efficiency was due to careful attention to detail in every part, improved wing sections, clean fuselage-lines, and simplified undercarriages. At the same time, in the early part of 1913 a tendency manifested itself towards the four-wheeled undercarriage, a pair of smaller wheels being added in front of the main wheels to prevent overturning while running on the ground; and several designs of oleo-pneumatic and steel-spring undercarriages were produced in place of the rubber shock-absorber type which had up till then been almost universal.

These two statements as to undercarriage designs may appear to be contradictory, but in reality they do not conflict as they both showed a greater attention to the importance of good springing, combined with a desire to avoid complication and a mass of struts and wires which increased head resistance.

The Olympia Aero Show of March, 1913, also produced a machine which, although the type was not destined to prove the best for the purpose for which it was designed, was of interest as being the first to be designed specially for war purposes. This was the Vickers 'Gun-bus,' a 'pusher' machine, with the propeller revolving behind the main planes between the outriggers carrying the tail, with a seat right in front for a gunner who was provided with a machine gun on a swivelling mount which had a free field of fire in every direction forward. The device which proved the death-blow for this type of aircraft during the war will be dealt with in the appropriate place later, but the machine should not go unrecorded.

As a result of a number of accidents to monoplanes the Government appointed a Committee at the end of 1912 to inquire into the causes of these. The report which was presented in March, 1913, exonerated the monoplane by coming to the conclusion that the accidents were not caused by conditions peculiar to monoplanes, but pointed out certain desiderata in aeroplane design generally which are worth recording. They recommended that the wings of aeroplanes should be so internally braced as to have sufficient strength in themselves not to collapse if the external bracing wires should give way. The practice, more common in monoplanes than biplanes, of carrying important bracing wires from the wings to the undercarriage was condemned owing to the liability of damage from frequent landings. They also pointed out the desirability of duplicating all main wires and their attachments, and of using stranded cable for control wires. Owing to the suspicion that one accident at least had been caused through the tearing of the fabric away from the wing, it was recommended that fabric should be more securely fastened to the ribs of the wings, and that devices for preventing the spreading of tears should be considered. In the last connection it is interesting to note that the French Deperdussin firm produced a fabric wing-covering with extra strong threads run at right-angles through the fabric at intervals in order to limit the tearing to a defined area.

In spite, however, of the whitewashing of the monoplane by the Government Committee just mentioned, considerable stir was occasioned later in the year by the decision of the War office not to order any more monoplanes; and from this time forward until the War period the British Army was provided exclusively with biplanes. Even prior to this the popularity of the monoplane had begun to wane. At the Olympia Aero Show in March, 1913, biplanes for the first time outnumbered the 'single-deckers'(as the Germans call monoplanes); which had the effect of reducing the wing-loading. In the case of the biplanes exhibited this averaged about 4 1/2 lbs. per square foot, while in the case of the monoplanes in the same exhibition the lowest was 5 1/2 lbs., and the highest over 8 1/2 lbs. per square foot of area. It may here be mentioned that it was not until the War period that the importance of loading per horse-power was recognised as the true criterion of aeroplane efficiency, far greater interest being displayed in the amount of weight borne per unit area of wing.

An idea of the state of development arrived at about this time may be gained from the fact that the Commandant of the Military Wing of the Royal Flying Corps in a lecture before the Royal Aeronautical Society read in February, 1913, asked for single-seater scout aeroplanes with a speed of 90 miles an hour and a landing speed of 45 miles an hour—a performance which even two years later would have been considered modest in the extreme. It serves to show that, although higher performances were put up by individual machines on occasion, the general development had not yet reached the stage when such performances could be obtained in machines suitable for military purposes. So far as seaplanes were concerned, up to the beginning of 1913 little attempt had been made to study the novel problems involved, and the bulk of the machines at the Monaco Meeting in April, 1913, for instance, consisted of land machines fitted with floats, in many cases of a most primitive nature, without other alterations. Most of those which succeeded in leaving the water did so through sheer pull of engine power; while practically all were incapable of getting off except in a fair sea, which enabled the pilot to jump the machine into the air across the trough between two waves. Stability problems had not yet been considered, and in only one or two cases was fin area added at the rear high up, to counterbalance the effect of the floats low down in front. Both twin and single-float machines were used, while the flying boat was only just beginning to come into being from the workshops of Sopwith in Great Britain, Borel-Denhaut in France, and Curtiss in America. In view of the approaching importance of amphibious seaplanes, mention should be made of the flying boat (or 'bat boat' as it was called, following Rudyard Kipling) which was built by Sopwith in 1913 with a wheeled landing-carriage which could be wound up above the bottom surface of the boat so as to be out of the way when alighting on water.

During 1913 the (at one time almost universal) practice originated by the Wright Brothers, of warping the wings for lateral stability, began to die out and the bulk of aeroplanes began to be fitted with flaps (or 'ailerons') instead. This was a distinct change for the better, as continually warping the wings by bending down the extremities of the rear spars was bound in time to produce 'fatigue' in that member and lead to breakage; and the practice became completely obsolete during the next two or three years.

The Gordon-Bennett race of September, 1913, was again won by a Deperdussin machine, somewhat similar to that of the previous year, but with exceedingly small wings, only 107 square feet in area. The shape of these wings was instructive as showing how what, from the general utility point of view, may be disadvantageous can, for a special purpose, be turned to account. With a span of 21 feet, the chord was 5 feet, giving the inefficient 'aspect ratio' of slightly over 4 to 1 only. The object of this was to reduce the lift, and therefore the resistance, to as low a point as possible. The total weight was 1,500 lbs., giving a wing-loading of 14 lbs. per square foot—a hitherto undreamt-of figure. The result was that the machine took an enormously long run before starting; and after touching the ground on landing ran for nearly a mile before stopping; but she beat all records by attaining a speed of 126 miles per hour. Where this performance is mainly interesting is in contrast to the machines of 1920, which with an even higher speed capacity would yet be able to land at not more than 40 or 50 miles per hour, and would be thoroughly efficient flying machines.

The Rheims Aviation Meeting, at which the Gordon-Bennett race was flown, also saw the first appearance of the Morane 'Parasol' monoplane. The Morane monoplane had been for some time an interesting machine as being the only type which had no fixed surface in rear to give automatic stability, the movable elevator being balanced through being hinged about one-third of the way back from the front edge. This made the machine difficult to fly except in the hands of experts, but it was very quick and handy on the controls and therefore useful for racing purposes. In the 'Parasol' the modification was introduced of raising the wing above the body, the pilot looking out beneath it, in order to give as good a view as possible.

Before passing to the year 1914 mention should be made of the feat performed by Nesteroff, a Russian, and Pegoud, a French pilot, who were the first to demonstrate the possibilities of flying upside-down and looping the loop. Though perhaps not coming strictly within the purview of a chapter on design (though certain alterations were made to the top wing-bracing of the machine for this purpose) this performance was of extreme importance to the development of aviation by showing the possibility of recovering, given reasonable height, from any position in the air; which led designers to consider the extra stresses to which an aeroplane might be subjected and to take steps to provide for them by increasing strength where necessary.

When the year 1914 opened a speed of 126 miles per hour had been attained and a height of 19,600 feet had been reached. The Sopwith and Avro (the forerunner of the famous training machine of the War period) were probably the two leading tractor biplanes of the world, both two-seaters with a speed variation from 40 miles per hour up to some 90 miles per hour with 80 horse-power engines. The French were still pinning their faith mainly to monoplanes, while the Germans were beginning to come into prominence with both monoplanes and biplanes of the 'Taube' type. These had wings swept backward and also upturned at the wing-tips which, though it gave a certain measure of automatic stability, rendered the machine somewhat clumsy in the air, and their performances were not on the whole as high as those of either France or Great Britain.

Early in 1914 it became known that the experimental work of Edward Busk—who was so lamentably killed during an experimental flight later in the year—following upon the researches of Bairstow and others had resulted in the production at the Royal Aircraft Factory at Farnborough of a truly automatically stable aeroplane. This was the 'R.E.' (Reconnaissance Experimental), a development of the B.E. which has already been referred to. The remarkable feature of this design was that there was no particular device to which one could point out as the cause of the stability. The stable result was attained simply by detailed design of each part of the aeroplane, with due regard to its relation to, and effect on, other parts in the air. Weights and areas were so nicely arranged that under practically any conditions the machine tended to right itself. It did not, therefore, claim to be a machine which it was impossible to upset, but one which if left to itself would tend to right itself from whatever direction a gust might come. When the principles were extended to the 'B.E. 2c' type (largely used at the outbreak of the War) the latter machine, if the engine were switched of f at a height of not less than 1,000 feet above the ground, would after a few moments assume its correct gliding angle and glide down to the ground.

The Paris Aero Salon of December, 1913, had been remarkable chiefly for the large number of machines of which the chassis and bodywork had been constructed of steel-tubing; for the excess of monoplanes over biplanes; and (in the latter) predominance of 'pusher' machines (with propeller in rear of the main planes) compared with the growing British preference for 'tractors' (with air screw in front). Incidentally, the Maurice Farman, the last relic of the old type box-kite with elevator in front appeared shorn of this prefix, and became known as the 'short-horn' in contradistinction to its front-elevatored predecessor which, owing to its general reliability and easy flying capabilities, had long been affectionately called the 'mechanical cow.' The 1913 Salon also saw some lingering attempts at attaining automatic stability by pendulum and other freak devices.

ABOUT THE AUTHOR

W. Lockwood Marsh and Evelyn Charles Vivian are distinguished authors renowned for their groundbreaking work, "A History of Aeronautics." This seminal masterpiece provides an exhaustive exploration of humanity's journey into the skies, tracing the evolution of flight from its earliest conceptualizations to the modern era of aviation. With meticulous research and captivating prose, Marsh and Vivian illuminate the pioneering efforts, technological advancements, and daring achievements that have shaped the field of aeronautics. Through comprehensive coverage of key milestones, groundbreaking inventions, and notable figures in aviation history, Marsh and Vivian offer readers a comprehensive understanding of the complex tapestry of human ingenuity and perseverance in conquering the skies. Their narrative skillfully navigates the intersection of science, technology, and human ambition, highlighting the triumphs and tribulations encountered in the pursuit of flight. "A History of Aeronautics" stands as a testament to Marsh and Vivian's dedication to chronicling the remarkable progress of aviation and its profound impact on society. This monumental work continues to inspire and inform aviation enthusiasts, historians, and scholars alike, ensuring its enduring legacy in the annals of aeronautical literature.

CONTENTS

FOREWORD 7

PART II
1903-1920: PROGRESS IN DESIGN

I THE BEGINNINGS 9

II MULTIPLICITY OF IDEAS 16

III PROGRESS ON STANDARDISED LINES 21

IV THE WAR PERIOD 28

FOREWORD

Although successful heavier-than-air flight is less than two decades old, and successful dirigible propulsion antedates it by a very short period, the mass of experiment and accomplishment renders any one-volume history of the subject a matter of selection. In addition to the restrictions imposed by space limits, the material for compilation is fragmentary, and, in many cases, scattered through periodical and other publications. Hitherto, there has been no attempt at furnishing a detailed account of how the aeroplane and the dirigible of to-day came to being, but each author who has treated the subject has devoted his attention to some special phase or section. The principal exception to this rule—Hildebrandt—wrote in 1906, and a good many of his statements are inaccurate, especially with regard to heavier-than-air experiment.

Such statements as are made in this work are, where possible, given with acknowledgment to the authorities on which they rest. Further acknowledgment is due to Lieut.-Col. Lockwood Marsh, not only for the section on aeroplane development which he has contributed to the work, but also for his kindly assistance and advice in connection with the section on aerostation. The author's thanks are also due to the Royal Aeronautical Society for free access to its valuable library of aeronautical literature, and to Mr A. Vincent Clarke for permission to make use of his notes on the development of the aero engine.

In this work is no claim to originality—it has been a matter mainly of compilation, and some stories, notably those of the Wright Brothers and of Santos Dumont, are better told in the words of the men themselves than any third party could tell them. The author claims, however, that this is the first attempt at recording the facts of development and stating, as fully as is possible in the compass of a single volume, how flight and aerostation have evolved. The time for a critical history of the subject is not yet.

In the matter of illustrations, it has been found very difficult to secure suitable material. Even the official series of photographs of aeroplanes in the war period is curiously incomplete' and the methods of censorship during that period prevented any complete series being privately collected. Omissions in this respect will probably be remedied in future editions of the work, as fresh material is constantly being located.

E.C.V. October, 1920.

PART II
1903-1920: PROGRESS IN DESIGN

By Lieut.-Col. W. Lockwood Marsh

I
THE BEGINNINGS

Although the first actual flight of an aeroplane was made by the Wrights on December 17th 1903, it is necessary, in considering the progress of design between that period and the present day, to go back to the earlier days of their experiments with 'gliders,' which show the alterations in design made by them in their step-bystep progress to a flying machine proper, and give a clear idea of the stage at which they had arrived in the art of aeroplane design at the time of their first flights.

They started by carefully surveying the work of previous experimenters, such as Lilienthal and Chanute, and from the lesson of some of the failures of these pioneers evolved certain new principles which were embodied in their first glider, built in 1900. In the first place, instead of relying upon the shifting of the operator's body to obtain balance, which had proved too slow to be reliable, they fitted in front of the main supporting surfaces what we now call an 'elevator,' which could be flexed, to control the longitudinal balance, from where the operator lay prone upon the main supporting surfaces. The second main innovation which they incorporated in this first glider, and the principle of which is still used in every aeroplane in existence, was the attainment of lateral balance by warping the extremities of the main planes. The effect of warping or pulling down the extremity of the wing on one side was to increase its lift and so cause that side to rise. In the first two gliders this control was also used for steering to right and left. Both these methods of control were novel for other than model work, as previous experimenters, such as Lilienthal and Pilcher, had relied entirely upon moving the legs or shifting the position of the body to control the longitudinal and lateral motions of their gliders. For the main supporting surfaces of the glider the biplane system of Chanute's gliders was adopted with certain modifications, while the curve of the wings was founded upon the calculations of Lilienthal as to wind pressure and consequent lift of the plane.

This first glider was tested on the Kill Devil Hill sand-hills in North Carolina in the summer of 1900 and proved at any rate the correctness of the principles of the front elevator and warping wings, though its designers were puzzled by the fact that the lift was less than they expected; whilst the 'drag'(as we call it), or resistance, was also considerably lower than their predictions. The 1901 machine was, in consequence, nearly doubled in area—the lifting surface being increased from 165 to 308 square feet—the first trial taking place on July 27th, 1901, again at Kill Devil Hill. It immediately appeared that something was wrong, as the machine dived straight to the ground, and it was only after the operator's position had been moved nearly a foot back from what had been calculated as the correct position that the machine would glide—and even then the elevator had to be used far more strongly than in the previous year's glider. After a good deal of thought the apparent solution of the trouble was finally found.

This consisted in the fact that with curved surfaces, while at large angles the centre of pressure moves forward as the angle decreases, when a certain limit of angle is reached it travels suddenly backwards and causes the machine to dive. The Wrights had known of this tendency from Lilienthal's researches, but had imagined that the phenomenon would disappear if they used a fairly lightly cambered—or curved—surface with a very abrupt curve at the front. Having discovered what appeared to be the cause they surmounted the difficulty by 'trussing down' the camber of the wings, with the result that they at once got back to the old conditions of the previous year and could control the machine readily with small movements of the elevator, even being able to follow undulations in the ground. They still found, however, that the lift was not as great as it should have been; while the drag remained, as in the previous glider, surprisingly small. This threw doubt on previous figures as to wind resistance and pressure on curved surfaces; but at the same time confirmed (and this was a most important result) Lilienthal's previously questioned theory that at small angles the pressure on a curved surface instead of being normal, or at right angles to, the chord is in fact inclined in front of the perpendicular. The result of this is that the pressure actually tends to draw the machine forward into the wind—hence the small amount of drag, which had puzzled Wilbur and Orville Wright.

Another lesson which was learnt from these first two years of experiment, was that where, as in a biplane, two surfaces are superposed one above the other, each of them has somewhat less lift than it would have if used alone.

The experimenters were also still in doubt as to the efficiency of the warping method of controlling the lateral balance as it gave rise to certain phenomena which puzzled them, the machine turning towards the wing having the greater angle, which seemed also to touch the ground first, contrary to their expectations. Accordingly, on returning to Dayton towards the end of 1901, they set themselves to solve the various problems which had appeared and started on a lengthy series of experiments to check the previous figures as to wind resistance and lift of curved surfaces, besides setting themselves to grapple with the difficulty of lateral control. They accordingly constructed for themselves at their home in Dayton a wind tunnel 16 inches square by 6 feet long in which they measured the lift and 'drag' of more than two hundred miniature wings. In the course of these tests they for the first time produced comparative results of the lift of oblong and square surfaces, with the result that they re-discovered the importance of 'aspect ratio'—the ratio of length to breadth of planes. As a result, in the next year's glider the aspect ration of the wings was increased from the three to one of the earliest model to about six to one, which is approximately the same as that used in the machines of to-day. Further than that, they discussed the question of lateral stability, and came to the conclusion that the cause of the trouble was that the effect of warping down one wing was to increase the resistance of, and consequently slow down, that wing to such an extent that its lift was reduced sufficiently to wipe out the anticipated increase in lift resulting from the warping. From this they deduced that if the speed of the warped wing could be controlled the advantage of increasing the angle by warping could be utilised as they originally intended. They therefore decided to fit a vertical fin at the rear which, if the machine attempted to turn, would be exposed more and more to the wind and so stop the turning motion by offering increased resistance.

As a result of this laboratory research work the third Wright glider, which was taken to Kill Devil Hill in September, 1902, was far more efficient aerodynamically than either of its two predecessors, and was fitted with a fixed vertical fin at the rear in addition to the movable elevator in front. According to Mr Griffith Brewer,[*] this third glider contained 305 square feet of surface; though there may possibly be a mistake here, as he states[**] the surface of the previous year's glider to have been only 290 square feet, whereas Wilbur Wright himself[***] states it to have been 308 square feet. The matter is not, perhaps, save historically, of much importance, except that the gliders are believed to have been progressively larger, and therefore if we accept Wilbur Wright's own figure of the surface of the second glider, the third must have had a greater area than that given by Mr Griffith Brewer. Unfortunately, no evidence of the Wright Brothers themselves on this point is available.

[*] Fourth Wilbur Wright Memorial Lecture, Aeronautical Journal, Vol. XX, No. 79, page 75.

[**] Ibid. page 73.

[***] Ibid. pp. 91 and 102.

The first glide of the 1902, season was made on September 17th of that year, and the new machine at once showed itself an improvement on its predecessors, though subsequent trials showed that the difficulty of lateral balance had not been entirely overcome. It was decided, therefore, to turn the vertical fin at the rear into a rudder by making it movable. At the same time it was realised that there was a definite relation between lateral balance and directional control, and the rudder controls and wing-warping wires were accordingly connected This ended the pioneer gliding experiments of Wilbur and Orville Wright—though further glides were made in subsequent years—as the following year, 1903, saw the first power-driven machine leave the ground.

To recapitulate—in the course of these original experiments the Wrights confirmed Lilienthal's theory of the reversal of the centre of pressure on cambered surfaces at small angles of incidence: they confirmed the importance of high aspect ratio in respect to lift: they had evolved new and more accurate tables of lift and pressure on cambered surfaces: they were the first to use a movable horizontal elevator for controlling height: they were the first to adjust the wings to different angles of incidence to maintain lateral balance: and they were the first to use the movable rudder and adjustable wings in combination.

They now considered that they had gone far enough to justify them in building a power-driven 'flier,' as they called their first aeroplane. They could find no suitable engine and so proceeded to build for themselves an internal combustion engine, which was designed to give 8 horse-power, but when completed actually developed about 12-15 horse-power and weighed 240 lbs. The complete machine weighed about 750 lbs. Further details of the first Wright aeroplane are difficult to obtain, and even those here given should be received with some caution. The first flight was made on December 17th 1903, and lasted 12 seconds. Others followed immediately, and the fourth lasted 59 seconds, a distance of 852 feet being covered against a 20-mile wind.

The following year they transferred operations to a field outside Dayton, Ohio (their home), and there they flew a somewhat larger anpower is one which should not be overlooked. The wing loading was about 1 1/2 lbs. per square foot.

Apart from the appearance of 'R.E.1,' perhaps the most notable development towards the end of 1913 was the appearance of the Sopwith 'Tabloid 'tractor biplane. This single-seater machine, evolved from the two-seater previously referred to, fitted with a Gnome engine of 80 horse-power, had the, for those days, remarkable speed of 92 miles an hour; while a still more notable feature was that it could remain in level flight at not more than 37 miles per hour. This machine is of particular importance because it was the prototype and forerunner of the successive designs of single-seater scout fighting machines which were used so extensively from 1914 to 1918. It was also probably the first machine to be capable of reaching a height of 1,000 feet within one minute. It was closely followed by the 'Bristol Bullet,' which was exhibited at the Olympia Aero Show of March, 1914. This last pre-war show was mainly remarkable for the good workmanship displayed—rather than for any distinct advance in design. In fact, there was a notable diversity in the types displayed, but in detailed design considerable improvements were to be seen, such as the general adoption of stranded steel cable in place of piano wire for the mail bracing.

IV
THE WAR PERIOD

Up to this point an attempt has been made to give some idea of the progress that was made during the eleven years that had elapsed since the days of the Wrights' first flights. Much advance had been made and aeroplanes had settled down, superficially at any rate, into more or less standardised forms in three main types—tractor monoplanes, tractor biplanes, and pusher biplanes. Through the application of the results of experiments with models in wind tunnels to full-scale machines, considerable improvements had been made in the design of wing sections, which had greatly increased the efficiency of aeroplanes by raising the amount of 'lift' obtained from the wing compared with the 'drag' (or resistance to forward motion) which the same wing would cause. In the same way the shape of bodies, interplane struts, etc., had been improved to be of better streamline shape, for the further reduction of resistance; while the problems of stability were beginning to be tolerably well understood. Records (for what they are worth) stood at 21,000 feet as far as height was concerned, 126 miles per hour for speed, and 24 hours duration. That there was considerable room for development is, however, evidenced by a statement made by the late B. C. Hucks (the famous pilot) in the course of an address delivered before the Royal Aeronautical Society in July, 1914. 'I consider,' he said, 'that the present day standard of flying is due far more to the improvement in piloting than to the improvement in machines.... I consider those (early 1914) machines are only slight improvements on the machines of three years ago, and yet they are put through evolutions which, at that time, were not even dreamed of. I can take a good example of the way improvement in piloting has outdistanced improvement in machines—in the case of myself, my 'looping' Bleriot. Most of you know that there is very little difference between that machine and the 50 horse-power Bleriot of three years ago.' This statement was, of course, to some extent an exaggeration and was by no means agreed with by designers, but there was at the same time a germ of truth in it. There is at any rate little doubt that the theory and practice of aeroplane design made far greater strides towards becoming an exact science during the four years of War than it had done during the six or seven years preceding it.

It is impossible in the space at disposal to treat of this development even with the meagre amount of detail that has been possible while covering the 'settling down' period from 1911 to 1914, and it is proposed, therefore, to indicate the improvements by sketching briefly the more noticeable difference in various respects between the average machine of 1914 and a similar machine of 1918.

In the first place, it was soon found that it was possible to obtain greater efficiency and, in particular, higher speeds, from tractor machines than from pusher machines with the air screw behind the main planes. This was for a variety of reasons connected with the efficiency of propellers and the possibility of reducing resistance to a greater extent in tractor machines by using a 'stream-line' fuselage (or body) to connect the main planes with the tail. Full advantage of this could not be taken, however, owing to the difficulty of fixing a machine-gun in a forward direction owing to the presence of the propeller. This was finally overcome by an ingenious device (known as an 'Interrupter gear') which allowed the gun to fire only when none of the propeller blades was passing in front of the muzzle. The monoplane gradually fell into desuetude, mainly owing to the difficulty of making that type adequately strong without it becoming prohibitively heavy, and also because of its high landing speed and general lack of manoeuvrability. The triplane was also little used except in one or two instances, and, practically speaking, every machine was of the biplane tractor type.

A careful consideration of the salient features leading to maximum efficiency in aeroplanes—particularly in regard to speed and climb, which were the two most important military requirements—showed that a vital feature was the reduction in the amount of weight lifted per horse-power employed; which in 1914 averaged from 20 to 25 lbs. This was effected both by gradual increase in the power and size of the engines used and by great improvement in their detailed design (by increasing compression ratio and saving weight whenever possible); with the result that the motive power of single-seater aeroplanes rose from 80 and 100 horse-power in 1914 to an average of 200 to 300 horse-power, while the actual weight of the engine fell from 3 1/2-4 lbs. per horse-power to an average of 2 1/2 lbs. per horse-power. This meant that while a pre-war engine of 100 horse-power would weigh some 400 lbs., the 1918 engine developing three times the power would have less than double the weight. The result of this improvement was that a scout aeroplane at the time of the Armistice would have 1 horse-power for every 8 lbs. of weight lifted, compared with the 20 or 25 lbs. of its 1914 predecessors. This produced a considerable increase in the rate of climb, a good postwar machine being able to reach 10,000 feet in about 5 minutes and 20,000 feet in under half an hour. The loading per square foot was also considerably increased; this being rendered possible both by improvement in the design of wing sections and by more scientific construction giving increased strength. It will be remembered that in the machine of the very early period each square foot of surface had only to lift a weight of some 1 1/2 to 2 lbs., which by 1914 had been increased to about 4 lbs. By 1918 aeroplanes habitually had a loading of 8 lbs. or more per square foot of area; which resulted in great increase in speed. Although a speed of 126 miles per hour had been attained by a specially designed racing machine over a short distance in 1914, the average at that period little exceeded, if at all, 100 miles per hour; whereas in 1918 speeds of 130 miles per hour had become a commonplace, and shortly afterwards a speed of over 166 miles an hour was achieved.

In another direction, also, that of size, great developments were made. Before the War a few machines fitted with more than one engine had been built (the first being a triple Gnome-engined biplane built by Messrs Short Bros. at Eastchurch in 1913), but none of large size had been successfully produced, the total weight probably in no case exceeding about 2 tons. In 1916, however, the twin engine Handley-Page biplane was produced, to be followed by others both in this country and abroad, which represented a very great increase in size and, consequently, load-carrying capacity. By the end of the War period several types were in existence weighing a total of 10 tons when fully loaded, of which some 4 tons or more represented 'useful load' available for crew, fuel, and bombs or passengers. This was attained through very careful attention to detailed design, which showed that the material could be employed more efficiently as size increased, and was also due to the fact that a large machine was not liable to be put through the same evolutions as a small machine, and therefore could safely be built with a lower factor of safety. Owing to the fact that a wing section which is adopted for carrying heavy loads usually has also a somewhat low lift to drag ratio, and is not therefore productive of high speed, these machines are not as fast as light scouts; but, nevertheless, they proved themselves capable of achieving speeds of 100 miles an hour or more in some cases; which was faster than the average small machine of 1914.

In one respect the development during the War may perhaps have proved to be somewhat disappointing, as it might have been expected that great improvements would be effected in metal construction, leading almost to the abolition of wooden structures. Although, however, a good deal of experimental work was done which resulted in overcoming at any rate the worst of the difficulties, metal-built machines were little used (except to a certain extent in Germany) chiefly on account of the need for rapid production and the danger of delay resulting from switching over from known and tried methods to experimental types of construction. The Germans constructed some large machines, such as the giant Siemens-Schukhert machine, entirely of metal except for the wing covering, while the Fokker and Junker firms about the time of the Armistice in 1918 both produced monoplanes with very deep all-metal wings (including the covering) which were entirely unstayed externally, depending for their strength on internal bracing. In Great Britain cable bracing gave place to a great extent to 'stream-line wires,' which are steel rods rolled to a more or less oval section, while tie-rods were also extensively used for the internal bracing of the wings. Great developments in the economical use of material were also made in the direction of using built-up main spars for the wings and interplane struts; spars composed of a series of layers (or 'laminations') of different pieces of wood also being used.

Apart from the metallic construction of aeroplanes an enormous amount of work was done in the testing of different steels and light alloys for use in engines, and by the end of the War period a number of aircraft engines were in use of which the pistons and other parts were of such alloys; the chief difficulty having been not so much in the design as in the successful heat-treatment and casting of the metal.

An important development in connection with the inspection and testing of aircraft parts, particularly in the case of metal, was the experimental application of X-ray photography, which showed up latent defects, both in the material and in manufacture, which would otherwise have passed unnoticed. This method was also used to test the penetration of glue into the wood on each side of joints, so giving a measure of the strength; and for the effect of 'doping' the wings, dope being a film (of cellulose acetate dissolved in acetone with other chemicals) applied to the covering of wings and bodies to render the linen taut and weatherproof, besides giving it a smooth surface for the lessening of 'skin friction' when passing rapidly through the air.

An important result of this experimental work was that it in many cases enabled designers to produce aeroplane parts from less costly material than had previously been considered necessary, without impairing the strength. It may be mentioned that it was found undesirable to use welded joints on aircraft in any part where the material is subjectto a tensile or bending load, owing to the danger resulting from bad workmanship causing the material to become brittle—an effect which cannot be discovered except by cutting through the weld, which, of course, involves a test to destruction. Written, as it has been, in August, 1920, it is impossible in this chapter to give any conception of how the developments of War will be applied to commercial aeroplanes, as few truly commercial machines have yet been designed, and even those still show distinct traces of the survival of war mentality. When, however, the inevitable recasting of ideas arrives, it will become evident, whatever the apparent modification in the relative importance of different aspects of design, that enormous advances were made under the impetus of War which have left an indelible mark on progress.

We have, during the seventeen years since aeroplanes first took the air, seen them grow from tentative experimental structures of unknown and unknowable performance to highly scientific products, of which not only the performances (in speed, load-carrying capacity, and climb) are known, but of which the precise strength and degree of stability can be forecast with some accuracy on the drawing board. For the rest, with the future lies—apart from some revolutionary change in fundamental design—the steady development of a now well-tried and well-found engineering structure.